THE RED BANDANNA TRAVEL BOOK

The Medicine of Traveling

By Joanne Socha

Dear Anne,
We seem to be on similar paths... inspiring others to heal through travel.
Thanks for all you do
- Joanne

Amabelle Publishing, United States of America

The Red Bandanna Travel Book: The Medicine of Traveling

Published by Amabelle Publishing
Manchester-by-the-Sea, Massachusetts, U.S.A.

Cover artwork by Carolyn Barnes, www.carrieandseash.com
Illustration of The Spiral Slice by Haley Brennan
Author photograph by Melissa Mahoney Photography, www.melissamahoney.com
Book design and layout by Anne Holt Design, www.anneholtdesign.com

SOCHA, JOANNE, Author
The Red Bandanna Travel Book
Joanne Socha

ISBN: 978-0692173909

Schools, companies, professional groups, clubs, and other organizations may qualify for special terms when ordering quantities of this title. For information, contact Amabelle Publishing, 15 Beach Street #202, Manchester-by-the-Sea, MA 01944.

This book is not intended to be a substitute for the medical advice of a licensed physician. The reader should consult with his/her doctor in any matters relating to his/her health as the author does not give medical advice or prescribe any course of treatment for medical issues. The author offers general information to help people in their personal search for health, and therefore the author and the publisher assume no responsibility for your actions.

This book is printed in the United States of America.

This travel planner is the intellectual property of:

____

Dedicated to Mom, who was always seeking her
"house on the hill"...

to Saiful, may he find his Banyan Tree to sit under
and enjoy his days,

and to Nick, Nate, and my husband for showing
me the world through their eyes of love.

CONTENTS

Introduction

IF YOU BUILD IT...

Why a travel planner? Why not just jot down a "bucket list," tack it on the refrigerator or your computer, and be done with it? Well, because there is a bit of magic in orchestrating your travels. Daydreams, blue sky dreams, and dreams at night...

They all swirl around in our imagination beckoning us to explore new worlds. Simply writing a list each New Year's Eve or declaring, "it's on my bucket list," doesn't necessarily bring you any closer to manifesting your travel desires.

This workbook is all about your backstory – the behind the scenes insights into your travel cravings. I will take you through the simple steps I use to make the travels of my clients materialize, and my own travels, too. The steps work because we use our inner compass to unearth the yearnings behind our desires, learning why we're drawn to particular places, and what variables we consider along the way. Then we stage a silent coup and actually schedule some trips.

Writing in this journal is the labyrinth leading to the realization of your travel dreams. Your musings can then be the launch pad for a vision board, reading materials, mapping a route, taking the concrete steps to learning a language, researching cultures, researching ancestry, and booking your flights! Before you know it, you'll be racing down the tarmac headed to your #1.

Chapter One

MY MAGIC WAND MOMENT

My travels began in the back of a station wagon, traversing the United States with my five siblings and parents. This was not glamping, which is perhaps why today I gravitate toward more luxurious modes of travel. Back then it wasn't about the "lodgings." Ours consisted of a huge orange tent and incredibly uncomfortable cots, often cobbled together late at night when we finally arrived at our campsite having invariably strayed from the beaten path. Keep in mind that these were the days before GPS. Yet, glamour aside, I can still remember the glow and smell of the lanterns as they sizzled and faded to black for the evening. Cue the stars.

There were always adventures, like the time out West when my brother became so hot in the tent that he decided to sleep under the stars. He awoke to find a cow literally standing over him.

Or the time that we lost our brakes on the Rocky Mountains descent. I lay in the back of the station wagon, praying that we would make it to the foot of the mountains. We did, but I think Mom aged ten years that day.

There was always a new discovery to be had when we pulled into camp. For instance, checking out the bathrooms was a must, along with seeing if there were kids in the 'hood,' running barefoot and free, and shoving off for the day in my father's motor boat to explore new waters. It was pure replenishment.

Then, there was my first European experience in my beloved France, a sort of rite of passage trip with my mother and sister. My mother is of French descent and longed for ages to go, and after I finished high school, we were off! Again, many adventures ensued. Like the time my sister and mother locked me out of our room, pushing me into the lobby of the hotel to say, "je desire les postcards" to the cute French guy behind the desk. This was my first introduction into cultural nuances!

After that, there was honeymoon #1 (one of three, in fact—hey, I love to travel!) to Venice and throughout Europe, and then solo trips to Spain and the Canary Islands. But then I shelved all my other travel dreams while I raised my sons. I remained a voracious reader and armchair traveler, and Nick, Nate and I did our share of exploring in the United States.

My travel turning point came when, as an attorney with my own lovely firm, a travel journalist asked me to settle a slip and fall case for her. She was so pleased with the result that she asked me to help her reposition her business into a full service travel agency. Her first mistake was sending me to Cannes to attend a luxury travel show. While there, I fell in love with the industry, deciding to leverage my skills and flee my life as a lawyer to become a luxury travel designer. Tables turned!

That trip launched me into a swirling, wonderful world of travel, one in which I create happy memories for clients, and slip into my three piece suit when needed to become a travel advocate. And that is my why.

Chapter Two

LET'S CURATE SOME CONTINENTS

You might be surprised to learn that I have yet to travel to Antarctica. I've been to Asia, Australia, Europe, North and South America, and Africa. But now that I've revealed that skeleton in my closet, let's look at each continent and see which one(s) you're drawn to, and why. Number them in order of preference and jot a few notes about the allure of each part of the world:

- Asia
- Australia
- Europe
- North America
- South America
- Africa
- Antarctica

And now some seas…

Why is it that the seas are so beautifully named?
What seas of the world have you dipped your toe into? Here are some I've seen and have yet to see…what about you? Circle which ones appeal and add your own:

- The Laptev (Nordenskjold) Sea
- The Norwegian Sea
- The Sea of the Hebrides
- The Baltic Sea
- The Sargasso Sea
- The Tyrrhenian Sea
- The Ionian Sea
- The Sea of Marmara
- The Thracian Sea
- The Sea of Crete
- The Java Sea
- The Coral Sea
- The Caspian Sea
- The Black Sea
- The Sea of Azov
- The Red Sea
- The Arabian Sea
- The East China Sea
- The Dead Sea
- The Yatsushiro Sea

Chapter Three

THE SPIRAL SLICE

Let's Blue Sky this thing and pretend that money and time are no object, and that there are no other obstacles holding us back (fear of flying, diaper changes, work deadlines, pets, etc.). Pretend that you can take one trip per season—it could be as short as a weekend jaunt to Newport, RI to see the mansions, or as long as a hike up one of the Seven Summits. Perhaps you long for a girls' getaway to Golden Door, or a gentlemen's trip to Japan to meet sumo wrestlers. The main thing is not to censor yourself. Take the time to dream it into being. Put some continents/countries/cities on paper. I like to do this with a cup of espresso and a globe. It's where the magic starts, so go with your gut.

The beginning of the travel pie is represented by a labyrinthine swirl, which maps the seasons, the years, and the destinations, connected from beginning to end. As the years and travels pass, they are connected by our personal central thread; the inner compass of why we travel.

The personal evolution we desire at the beginning of our

journey is perceived all along the chart and then again at the end. The chart is meant to serve as a record of two parallel channels. The first channel is our concrete travel desires. The second channel is that part of our nature that's impossible to fully record: the spirit.

The spiral suggests harmony, moving forward on a wheel where 'slices' can be visited again through memory. Within the chart is endless freedom of choice.

Let's begin...

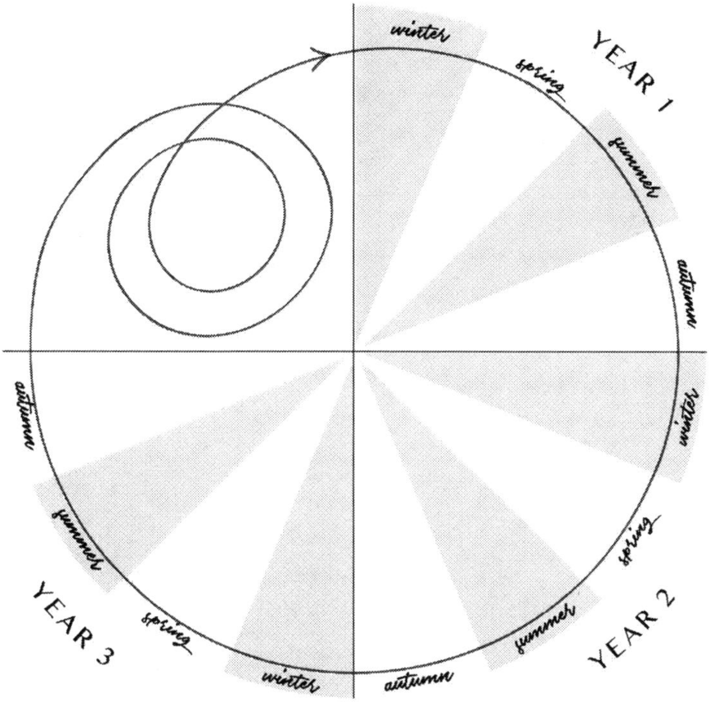

YEAR 1
winter
spring
summer
autumn
YEAR 2
winter
spring
summer
autumn
YEAR 3
winter
spring
summer
autumn

Chapter Four

HEADQUARTERS: THE WORLD

Doing this exercise will give you insight into why you love to travel, what you hope to achieve when doing so (relaxation, feasting on architectural sights, etc.), the goal of the trip, and your travel style (solo, small group, spouse or partner, en famille, large group). Just think about your daily life. What brings you pink thoughts and warm fuzzies?

If you haven't traveled much, think of places you enjoy spending time in your off-the-clock life. The sea? The opera? Your gym? To a meditation class?

SOME OF MY FAVORITE PLACES	THE WHY
My local bookstore	I become friends with fictional characters and dream about faraway lands.
France	Croissants and butter, the language, architecture, slipper moon over La Seine, hung just so.
Maldives	The Indian Ocean, romance, and uninhibited, starry, majestic skies.

Chapter Five

MRS. COURAGEOUS

My mom was an incredible mentor and muse. She was called Mrs. Courageous in a newspaper article published in The Journal-American. You see, she saved her six kids from a runaway truck (I was the tiniest at 3, in the back of the truck); she laid down her life for her children, going on to surmount other obstacles, big and little, thrown in her way. The New York Mirror was right when they headlined "Mom Lost Leg, But Not Heart."

I still marvel at how with one leg, on crutches, she would traverse the sand in North Truro, Cape Cod to swim in the bay. Nothing would stop her from taking a dip in her first love, the sea. People on their towels always stared in awe—back then having a handicap carried a severe stigma. They always came up and said, "Your mom is amazing."

"I know," I would shyly reply, my heart bursting.

If they only knew what a heroine she was. Sadly, her wooden leg was unlike the prosthetics of today—it was basically a carved piece of hard wood that she never once complained about putting on. Her cheery disposition earned her the nickname "Bubbles."

With Bubbles as my inspiration, I try to squarely face obstacles put in my path that might prevent me from accomplishing my dreams. And when it comes to travel dreams, it can be so easy to defer them. The excuses are plentiful: "I'll do it next year," "We can't afford it," "I don't deserve it," "I don't want to go alone," "I don't speak the language," "Paris will always be there"...

I've had my share of unfortunate events, but as General Patton declared, "Success is how high you bounce when you hit bottom."

These events have shaped me, and perhaps propelled me into making my career change, so I could share with others the happiness that was so generously passed on to me. My mother held back a truck for me—I have a purpose to fulfill, and I will do so! Looking at what I'm made of gives me an appreciation for the waters I've navigated. Let's spend a moment looking at hurdles cleared....it'll remind you how worthy you are, and help you start plotting your travel vision.

Some trials I encountered, confronted, and surmounted:

1. Critical illness of a spouse
2. Divorce (twice)

Your turn...

Chapter Six

WHO DO YOU WANT TO BE?

I'm always bumping into people who inspire me, and in the most far flung places! Invariably, whether I meet someone on a plane, on a ship, or at my local gym, the ones who lure me in all possess the same qualities: a love of learning about cultures, a thirst for new adventures, and a willingness to try unfamiliar things. They seek the little (and sometimes not so little) wonders.

Let's do this exercise to see who inspires you and why. Knowing the why will help you understand why you like to travel.

I'll start:

My Mom inspired me because she studied French every night after dinner at the kitchen table, hoping that she would be able to go to France and test her skills. And she did.

Lin, whom I met in South Africa, inspires me because at 74, she is still incredibly excited to go out into the local communities, learn about apartheid and the history of SA, go into the neighborhoods, meet with tribes, and open heartedly try to figure out what makes the country run.

Who inspires you?

Chapter Seven

TRAVEL AS MEDICINE

It seemed like I had ten years of distress in a row, but of course there were beautiful moments and memories generously sprinkled therein, especially the ones with my sons. But a change happened that caused me to question everything about myself when I witnessed something on the Metro North train out of New York City.

When the train stopped in New Rochelle, a young woman jumped off the train and onto the tracks from the elevated platform. She extended her arms like Christ on the cross and challenged the next train to hit her. Two thoughts came to mind: first, why would everyone immediately pull out their phones to document such a terrible moment, a plea for help, just so they could be first to post it on Instagram, Twitter or Facebook? The second was far more disturbing. I asked myself how someone could reach such a depth of despair to want to end her life. A chill straight down to my bones overcame me, because I realized that several years ago, I was that woman. There was a point during my former husband's protracted illness when I wanted to simply drive my car into the Housatonic

River and wait for it to slowly sink, the car filling with cold, black water.

I felt the same despair, albeit much briefer, when my family of origin ostracized me because of a modest inheritance from an aunt with whom I was particularly close. I may be the only sober WASP who has ever been kicked out of a family funeral. All this was very painful on the heels of the beautiful things that the priest had just said about family and love; an event I attended to pay homage to my family, our parents, our past, my Aunt, my Uncle, my heritage.

But I decided I didn't want to play the victim. Though I had been in the trenches, I was determined to pull myself out, to treat others with justice, kindness and love, knowing well that we are all in the trenches at one point or another. I wanted to know that, should someone be in a precarious situation, I would behave in a distinguished, gentle manner, and not treat them so badly that they wanted to jump onto the tracks.

My resuscitation came through travel. On one of the first hotel inspections I performed for the travel journalist, I met Stella, the owner of Rock Hall Luxe. Stella is an incredible jewelry designer who lives in Istanbul part-time. Over a lunch of heirloom tomatoes with figs and feta cheese, she described the exotic spices at the Grand Bazaar, the Old Silk Road, how you could have coffee in Europe and lunch in Asia, and how the Bosphorous Bridge twinkles at night. This was what I call my "confetti moment." I knew I had to go to Istanbul to experience it, and I also knew that I could spin this very magic for clients. Within three months, I was on Turkish Air headed for Istanbul and Cappadocia, where I inspected hotels, met with guides, explored restaurants and other travel-related services.

That trip saved me from my own train tracks; not literally, but it infused new hope and life back into me. That is my goal for you, if you need it.

What are your dark moments? Will you squarely face them and use them to propel you into self-healing? Travel can be your lifeline. Let's take a moment to list some sorrows that we may need to move on from. Not as victims, but to take another look at them and see if we can become the Mrs. Courageous of our stories.

Chapter Eight

THE GLOBAL MILKMAN STORY

When I was tiny, my mother used to tell us the story of an old-fashioned milkman', who rode along in his horse drawn cart and delivered milk, eggs and butter to families across the land, so that when they awoke, they would open their doors and behold: fresh eggs, milk, cream and butter!

She always started the story by making the sound of the horse's hooves on the pavement, describing the early morning fog, the determined milkman, and his weary but faithful horse, trudging through rain and snow to deliver yummy goods.

The milkman traveled around the globe! First he stopped at Joanne's house, leaving only milk and eggs, because she didn't need butter that day. He would often linger at her house for a cuppa, telling my mom all about what Dashiell in NJ was doing, what Sofia in Italy was doing, and what Sven in Sweden was doing.

Then the horse's hooves would click along the pavement to Dashiell's house in New Jersey, where an extra order of eggs, milk and butter was required, because Mama Anne was making cookies for the neighbors.

Somehow, he managed to cross oceans and mountains around the world to deliver fresh milk! What I love about the story is that it sparked my imagination in so many ways—my love of horses and their sounds and smells, the fresh cream on the doorstep, the loyal milkman, always appearing with shining eyes and tales of the others on his route. And his travels – there was the Silk Road Route, the Orient Express Route, the Camino Walk...never the same route twice in a row.

These are my earliest travel memories of a world without borders.

What are your earliest childhood travel memories that you can call to mind and savor right now? It is time for your milkman story – hopefully you can weave the tale for your children, if you have them, or for your inner child. Sigh, we were all young once. Don't forget the sound of the horse's hooves on the cobblestones!

What is your milkman story? Who would you like to visit around the world?

Chapter Nine

STAR OF THE SEA: COLLECTING MOMENTS

When I was in the Maldives scuba diving with my husband and a local guide who showed us the clearest spots of overabundant sea life, I learned two lessons:

The first I call the "circle fish twist." The circle fish were huge, flat, grey fish swimming around and around in a circle—a colony of about 30 fish. They were so serene and graceful that they reminded me of my ballerina days. When the rays of sun hit one at a time through the water, it seemed like that was their moment to shine. You could see their clear blue eyes transfixed, almost imperceptibly pausing in the sun as if this was their Oscar night moment. It reminded me to stop and relax and just be. I invoke the image whenever I need to be transported into serenity.

Another lesson occurred during the same tour, when I swam underwater ahead of my husband. He tapped me on the shoulder, waving his arms and urging me to circle back. He vigorously pointed out a huge shell on the bottom of the ocean floor—an oyster shell with megalomania. Its mother of pearl underbelly radiated rainbow colors back to me.....but the pearl was missing!

I'm so grateful that he pointed this shell out to me. To think I almost missed it! For me, the lesson is that we need others. We can miss beautiful things if left to our own devices. For months I wondered about that shell. Where was the pearl? After long reflection, I decided that I am the pearl. Not in a conceited, grandiose way, but to claim my own worth after intense heartache, establishing my connection to the sea and its inhabitants, to God, to the water, the sun, the perfection of the moon and stars, to love—it is all a great big circle of connection and I play a part in it.

What moments have you collected before in your travels... or which ones do you hope to collect? I think the moments themselves illuminate what we're seeking in our own lives.

Chapter Ten

PEARL OF THE SEA: YOU!

Confucius said "where you go, there you are," which means that no matter what we have going on at home, we can't escape it, because we take it with us—the worries, the problems, our behaviors, the deadlines, and so forth.

So I have a rule: when the plane is racing down the runway, I place my cares and worries into a red bandanna, tie it to a stick and drop it on the tarmac, leaving it there for the duration of the trip. It works! Then I am clear and free to experience the new lessons awaiting me at my destination. They aren't always tied up in a bright red bow either, but I never want to miss the reason I am called on the trip in the first place. Sometimes the lessons move me to tears, like the time I flew over Milford Sound in New Zealand in a helicopter. Before this point I was terrified of helicopters. Nevertheless, I totally surrendered to the moment, and the view was so stunning that I cried.

Other lessons are more painful. In Ringha, China (two valleys from Tibet), I saw an old woman with a sack of potatoes on her back, bent over, working from morning until night. No sight of the men. At first, I was angered by this sight (perhaps rightly so), but the message to me is to avoid being an officious intermeddler in another's cultural norms. How can we share the joy of what we've seen, and the sorrows, to make a dent in the world around us? When I saw the woman in the autonomous Tibetan prefecture laden down with the heavy sack of potatoes, I was filled with sorrow and wanted to right the wrongs for women around the world. But I had to come to terms that our culture is very different, and who am I to think mine is better? I did come back determined to inspire women to stand up for themselves.

So many of the lessons we need to learn in life don't come from books, but rather from living. That's why I love travel. I always glean incredible insights about myself that push me to become a better person. A work in progress!

What about you? What can you leave behind on your next trip, so you can be open to all that there is to learn once you have arrived? Treasure yourself.

Here are some things I am leaving behind on my next trip:

- My bullet journal
- My fear of Dobermans
- My fear of truly unusual foods

Chapter Eleven

PICASSO MOMENTS

When I went to Madrid with a group of travel consultants to inspect hotels, meet with guides, and learn about the city, one of the activities was a tour of the Prado Museum with a private guide. Now, I love museums, and I love art. But on this particular day wasn't "feeling it"—I would have preferred to linger in my glorious hotel room, lounging in my 1000 thread count sheets, and then soaking in the tub with tea and bubbles. I was still jet-lagged from the night before.

I reluctantly joined the group, but what ensued was a life-changing day for me. I had seen the painting of Las Meninas by Diego Velazquez countless times since my youth. I had stared at it for hours as a child, never knowing why I was drawn to it. But upon seeing it in person, I was bewitched. Of course, volumes have been written about the painting and its subjects, but for me it was all about The Infanta Margarita Maria and her presence. She was five at the time, but it looked as if she knew she was going to be forever immortalized in the painting. She was supposed to have become Queen. If you don't know the painting, please look it up. I realized at that moment that all my sadness and all my sorrows could recede into the shadows, and I could step into my personal moment in time. I simply had to claim it. The guide described the painting to us in such detail that it came alive. And then later, when we went to the Picasso Museum in Barcelona, I saw how Picasso had made her a Queen after all....

So now when I travel I always try new experiences, whether it be a guided tour at a new museum or a food I haven't eaten before.

What new things are you open to trying on your travels?

I'll go first:

1. I tried a helicopter ride (overcoming a lifelong fear of helicopters).
2. My friend and fellow lawyer turned travel designer, Saiful, tried bungee jumping. Saiful was the quietest of the pack of us travelling in New Zealand. One day we went to the original bungee jumping place. Saiful strode over to the jump point and was fitted with the cord. No one had seen him wander away...I just remember seeing Saiful jump off the bridge out of the corner of my eye. Who knew! We were all shocked, but not me. When I saw Saiful hanging upside down at the bottom, arms outstretched with life and seizing the moment, I understood that he had challenged himself, and the result for him was indescribable.

Chapter Twelve

TAKEOUT TRAVEL

If you could go into a shop and say, "I'll have one order of France, with a side of Prague, and for desert I think I'll try a quick stop in Iceland," and the itinerary was delivered to your door, all set for you—all details taken care of—and all you had to do was get on the plane, how would you feel? Some people would absolutely adore it. Not having to think about a thing, just showing up on the tarmac and gliding into the waiting jet.

Others would hate this method, as it takes away their creative input and drive for going on the trip in the first place. It's helpful to figure out your trip planning style to see how much time you can and want to reasonably devote to planning.

How would you like to design your trips? Pouring over travel guides in your local bookstore, scouring the internet for every deal possible? Reading novels and non-fiction books and articles, stuffing your head with ideas? Binging on Rick Steeves or another travel channel? Watching movies filmed in foreign lands? Pumping others for information after they return from their travels?

Personally, I am so busy planning for others that I don't have much time left to design my own trips (shoemaker's children have no shoes...), so I like to pick a partner I've collaborated with for a client's trip and enlist their assistance. Since I usually work right up until I'm on the plane, most of my reading about a place is done on the way to my destination. I am always happily surprised to learn on the way there. Then I get to broaden my perspective even further once on the ground: the big reveal!

Let's take a moment to brainstorm about the planning process and what works best for you. Knowing this information will enable you to get assistance if you need it or desire it:

After the inception of the trip idea I (circle what resonates, add your own):

- Head to a bookstore to read about a region
- Watch a couple of shows
- Spend hours on the internet reading reviews, maps, and various articles
- Talk to anybody who will listen about my plan
- Just obsess
- Call my travel consultant

Now, list five things you can do to start moving in the direction of the first destination on your chart. Let's jot down some steps—I'll go first:

I want to go to Morocco. I will:

1. Research the destination: go to a bookstore, talk to a friend who was there recently, and brainstorm with travel partners for more information.
2. Figure out my travel budget and the best time to go.
3. See if I can incorporate a milestone event (birthday celebration or anniversary)?
4. Decide how I want to see the country (camel, camping, Riad stays).
5. What do I want to learn while there? Cuisine? History?

Chapter Thirteen

READING ROOM RANDOMS

Books (and poems) that made me yearn for places. There are so many, but I'll list my top twenty, then you list yours:

1. Justine, by Laurence Durrell
2. The Magic Mountain, by Thomas Mann
3. Jane Eyre, by Jane Austen
4. The Bunny Planet, by Rosemary Wells
5. The Road To France, by Ina Caro
6. Ithaka, by C.P. Cavafy
7. A Separate Peace, by John Knowles
8. Siddhartha, by Herman Hesse
9. The Iliad, by Homer
10. The Odyssey, by Homer
11. Anna Karenina, by Leo Tolstoy
12. The Brothers Karamazov, by Leo Tolstoy
13. Remains of the Day, Kazuo Ishuguro
14. Cheri, by Colette

15. Romeo and Juliet, William Shakespeare
16. Rebecca, by Daphne Du Maurier
17. A Country Life, by Rachel Cusk
18. A View of Fuji, John Goodwin
19. Feast At The Beach, by William Widmaier
20. The Bible

Chapter Fourteen

CONFETTI TRAVEL MOMENTS

My top confetti travel moments so far (travel talk):

- Namibia and the world's oldest desert, persimmon colored
- Climbing the Patscherkofel
- Milford Sound via helicopter
- Visiting a Tibetan Farmhouse in Ringha, China
- Japanese Tea Ceremony in centuries-old teahouse in Kyoto, Japan
- Climbing the Red Rocks in Sedona, Arizona
- Sunset over a glacier in Iceland
- Picnic on top of a glacier in New Zealand
- Watching male flamenco dancers in Andalusia
- The Bells of Seville pealing
- The view from Museum Hotel in Cappadocia, Turkey

Sketch yours (or experiences that you would like to have)!

Chapter Fifteen

NORTHERN LIGHTS PERSPECTIVE

Travel advisors are constantly circling the globe to inspect hotels, meet guides, experience activities, and discover hidden finds for our clients. Investing in my business has always been a priority. While we do experience industry rates at many properties around the world, sometimes I travel on a dime so I can be totally anonymous and see how I am treated when no one is watching.

Plus, my budget doesn't always afford the ability to fly business class. When I recently went to Paris during Fashion Week and Berlin for a Healing Hotels Conference in March, I asked my husband to secure flights for me. Since he is the air specialist, I turned it over to him, knowing he would find the best flights. Imagine my surprise when he announced that I would be flying WOW Air via Reykjavik on my way to Paris.

I was barking mad on my way to the airport, complaining to him endlessly. When we arrived at Logan, I angrily snapped, "everyone is flying directly to Paris, but noooo, not me. I have to layover in Iceland!" He took it all in stride—he really was being a good sport. Anytime I travel without him, he takes me to the airport and waits with me until I go through security. I think that is just the sweetest thing ever. So I finally bit my tongue and said goodbye.

The WOW experience turned out to be a wonderful deviation! The plane was brand new, and it was practically empty, so I had three seats free to spread out and read and nap. Almost to Iceland, I awoke to a woman crying and saying, "Oh my God. Oh my God. I don't believe it." The pilot came on the intercom and said, "We are one hour out of Reykjavik. If you go to the left side of the plane you will be treated to a Northern Lights show."

Because I have been chasing the Northern Lights for years, most particularly in Iceland for the last two, I quickly darted to the left side of the plane. I could not believe the incredible beauty and feast for my eyes. The greens, the blues, the swirling magic and diamond stars thrown in the mix. I cried.

From now on, when my husband puts me on a flight anywhere, I am going to say, "okay, dear." Well, at least that's what I plan to say. Of course, I had to apologize to him and thank him profusely when I arrived home. Imagine what I would have missed if I hadn't taken that flight! That is the magic of travel: seeing the unexpected. The moments that make you freeze in your tracks and forget who, what, where, when and why. You're simply just a part of it all.

Chapter Sixteen

GENIE IN THE BOTTLE

I hereby grant that all your travel wishes shall come true, now that you have uncovered any blocks and obstacles in your way. Since you know why and where you want to go, what you want to do when you get there, and how you want to feel, it's time to get some globes! Let them swirl. Set some clocks to time zones around the world. Grab a map and some pins. Read National Geographic, travel books, and watch travel shows and talk to fellow travelers.

Gift travel to one another. Take a sample flying lesson. Give someone a seashell, a red rock from Sedona, AZ or a subscription to a travel magazine. Give a gorgeous photograph or a passport cover. Jump out of a plane with someone!

Discover Your World! Then share it!

And as a parting thought, I will wish you what I always wish for those I care about when they embark on a trip:

"Calm Sea and Prosperous Voyage" - Felix Mendelssohn

ABOUT THE AUTHOR

After a satisfying career as an attorney working with small start-ups and a Fortune 500 company, Joanne Socha turned the tables and entered the travel industry. She is a luxury travel advisor and the founder of Travel Far and Well, a Virtuoso-affiliated travel design firm catering to a diverse clientele. A world-class traveler, Joanne is also a speaker and a coach. She has used her trips as a healing medicine for the heart and mind, and strives to package restorative surprises into every journey she creates. Her mission is to help others heal and fall in love with the world.

Joanne is originally from South Salem, NY. She currently lives in New England with her family yet considers the world her headquarters.

Visit Joanne at www.joannesocha.com. Sign up for Joanne's monthly newsletter containing travel inspiration and the latest on wellness travel at www.travelfarandwell.com.

Joanne is also available for speaking engagements. To hire her for your next event please contact joanne@joannesocha.com.

43352006R00057

Made in the USA
Middletown, DE
24 April 2019